HER VOICE - ARTICLES ON WOMEN EMPOWERMENT TOWARDS A PROGRESSIVE NATION

DR. JAYA CHERIAN DR. RENI FRANCIS

ISBN 979-888629202-2

This book is dedicated to all women for their tireless, selfless and valuable contribution to the family, neighbourbood and society.

"There is no limit to what we, as women, can accomplish"
Michelle Obama

https://www.careerindia.com/features/international-women-s-day-inspirational-quotes-for-students-026413.html

Contents

CHAPTER ONE

SHE AND WE

Dr. Reni Francis

Principal

MES's Pillai College of Education and Research, Chembur

Women constitute 46.2 percent of the total enrolment in higher education but the female labour force participation rate is a mere 27 percent. Women form only 24 percent of entry-level professionals, out of which about 19 percent reach senior-level management roles and, yet, paid 20 percent less salaries than men. The aim of gender sensitization to make people aware of the power relations between men and women in society and to understand the importance of affording women and men equally opportunities and treatment. It's a strategy for making women's as well as men's concern & experience an integral dimension of the design, implementation, monitoring &

evaluation of polices so that equality is generated and inequality is not perpetuated.

Obstacles to Making a Gender Sensitive Organisation :

There are certain obstacles that prevent us from making our own organization more gender sensitive:

- There is insufficient awareness (of gender and other aspects of diversity) among staff in organizations; gender issues are still widely understood as women's issues only.
- Power relations between men and women in our own organizations are unequal in many ways , not just in terms of gender parity in staffing.
- Women do not have enough male allies in their organizations – indeed the interviews reveal residual male fear and resentment of any attempts to change gender relations.
- However, women themselves may bear some responsibility for isolating gender in organizations.
- As gender experts, we may create resistance by monopolizing gender issues, disempowering potential allies including men, or mystifying gender issues with jargon or heavily charged language.
- We need to 'sell' the idea of gender in our organizations (and with counterparts) via dialogue rather than antagonizing or mystifying.
- It is also important to emphasize the opportunities for change rather than concentrating only on finding and countering resistance.

Essential Features to Make an Organization Gender Sensitive :

- Gender equality should be a priority not only in the organization's mission statement, general objectives, and policies, but also in its internal regulations (recruitment procedures, terms and conditions for workers, etc.)
- Adequate resources should be devoted to putting such policies into practice.
- Accountability to women should be written into the organization's policies and carried out in its practice.
- There should be greater parity in numbers and distribution of staff, more – importantly, women on the staff and especially in management must be committed to gender equality. This means not feminine management, but feminist management, understood as management (by both sexes) that is committed to women's empowerment

- Since some degree of hierarchy is inevitable in any but very small organizations, this should be offset by a style of management that is open to change and oriented towards training, support, good feedback, and stimulating colleagues.
- Management-staff relations should be as non-vertical as possible: open, consultative, listening
- The organization should offer non-gender-stereotyped roles and choices for both men and women.
- There should be space for, and encouragement of, bottom-up initiatives and informal, 'horizontal' for ideas and dialogue.
- There should be scope for different organizational styles and cultures to coexist and be valued and for men and women together to explore and utilize difference without disempowering either side.

- Management should give unequivocal support to gender teams and staff members with specific responsibility for gender issues.
- Decision-making access for women should be built into the organization's structures, not dependent on informal agreements or arrangements, so that women's access to decision-making does not depend on the personalities and efforts of individuals.
- The organization should be one in which not only women, but everyone feels happy; one in which most people's best qualities are stimulated and recognized.

It is not about idolizing or victimizing any gender, It is about blending to achieve a goal.

References:

- Barodia, Shailly (2015). Gender Sensitization and Education, International Journal of Interdisciplinary and Multidisciplinary Studies, 2(4), pp. 107-113.
- Bharadwajh, Sree Krishna (2015). Laws Protecting Women from Gender Discrimination in India - A Critical Analysis. PARIPEX - Indian Journal of Research, 4(9), pp. 74-79.
- Bhasin, Kamla, (2004). Gender Basics, Exploring Masculinity, Delhi: Women Unlimited.
- Bhog, Dipta (2002). Gender and Curriculum. Economic and Political Weekly, 27th April, 37 (17). P.1638-1642
- G. Vijayeshwari Rao, (2004). Women and Society, Himalaya Publishing House, New Delhi.
- Gingine, A. P. and Narayanrao, AndhaleSarika (2016)Role of teacher in Gender Sensitivity, CnR's International Journal of Social & Scientific Research: Special Issue, 02 Special issue, (I),April, pp. 12-16.

- Gove J. and Watt S. (2004) Identity and Gender in K. Woodwarth (2nd Ed.) Questioning identity: Gender, Class, ethnicity, New York: Routledge.
- Jha, Priti& Nagar, Niti (2015). A Study of Gender Inequality in India, The International Journal of Indian Psychology, 2(3), April to June, pp. 46-53.
- John, Mary E. (Ed.) (2008). Women's Studies in India: A Reader, New Delhi: Penguin.
- NCERT (2006). National Focus Group on Gender Issues in Education (Position Paper), New Delhi.

CHAPTER TWO

Gender Equality-Empowering the other half of the Nation Builders

Dr. Jaya Cherian

Asst. Professor

MES's Pillai College of Education and Research, Chembur

As we celebrate International Women's Day on the 8th of March to appreciate and honor the accomplishments of women in various fields, it is also the time to focus on the challenges and the work still ahead in terms of achieving true equality for women. Giant strides have been made by women in various spheres whether social, political, cultural, economic, technological, science etc. We have women role models in almost every field and their accomplishments have inspired many others to similar achievements. As stated by the late Ruth Bader Ginsburg, Associate Justice of the Supreme Court of the United States, the second woman to serve on the Supreme Court- "As women achieve power, the barriers will fall. As society sees what women can do, as women see what women can do, there will be more women out there doing things, and we'll all be better off for it."

The meritorious achievements reached by women have been many a times in the face of great challenges, working in systems that have inbuilt biases against the female gender. These biases are sometimes explicit and obvious and many a times they are implicit and not really visible, yet they are there and experienced by women all over in different ways. The bias is displayed in the form of rules or customs or actions that discriminate against women or general ideas about women that stereotype and limit them into certain roles and levels of achievement. To remove this bias from our systems society needs to empower women.

Empowering women means that she has the power to make decisions and live her life as per her choices to live to her full potential, live a meaningful and fulfilling life. One of the key aspects of women empowerment is that it can take place only when women are made full partners in the decision-making process and her voice is heard where rules and policies are framed, where changes are being made in existing systems and where new systems are being shaped. As a nation we have a rich heritage of women leadership and achievements in contributing to the growth of our nation and yet there is much more that needs to be done. For our nation to attain its full potential we need to give equal partnership to the other half of the population- the women. Gender equality can be achieved through empowering women. By empowering women, we are ensuring the progress of our nation by providing the opportunity for development of all human resources and fulfilling the ideals of equality as envisioned in our Constitution. This need not be a vague dream for the future but a present reality through the sustained efforts of all of us a community.

Some of the ways in which women empowerment can be fostered include the following:

- Education is a key aspect of women empowerment, and it is crucial that society must harness all its resources towards providing access to education for women from all strata and providing them with the opportunities to developing their skills and talents.
- Women's representation and their presence in decision making bodies is essential so that their voice is heard, and their views form a part of the decisions that are made for their development.
- Capacity building opportunities should be provided in different areas so that women can upgrade their knowledge and skills and find opportunities in the job arena especially in a technology driven world. This will help them to overcome the gaps in their job skills as more often women stay out of this sector to focus on

family and home.

- Financial assistance and support systems that will help women entrepreneurship should be promoted especially in an economic system that is geared towards male entrepreneurship.
- Support systems in the form of leaves, work policies, care systems to help working mothers need to be devised and made a regular part of all work arenas.
- Women's health and nutrition needs to be emphasized and measures taken to bring focus on this much neglected aspect in all levels of society.
- Awareness programmes through the efforts of civil society, cultural organization, non-government organizations, media etc can help in changing the perceptions about the roles of men and women in society and create a more positive atmosphere conducive to women empowerment.
- Mentoring programmes needs to be promoted to provide guidance and support to young girls and women so that they can move forward in their chosen areas of work.

A society in which all individuals are treated equally is possible only when everyone both men and women believe in this and work towards this. Though we have the ideals, rules and policies what is needed is the will and determination to bring these ideals to fruition. As noted by the great freedom fighter, poet and the first woman governor of an Indian state, Sarojini Naidu- "We want deeper sincerity of motive, a greater courage in speech, and earnestness in action."

References:

- https://www.unfpa.org/resources/issue-7-women-empowerment
- https://www.un.org/sustainabledevelopment/gender-equality/
- https://opportunity.org/news/blog/2017/03/empowered-women-change-the-world
- https://kidadl.com/articles/best-female-empowerment-quotes-to-inspire-you
- https://www.iforher.com/quotes/famous-people/sarojini-naidu-quotes-national-womens-day-of-india/

CHAPTER THREE

Women Empowerment towards a Progressive Nation

Ms. Bharti Paryani

Alumna Batch: 2019-21

The woman is the builder and moulder of a nation's destiny. She is the supreme inspiration for man's onward march. – Rabindranath Tagore

Gender equality is first and foremost a human right. Empowering women is also a crucial tool for the advancing nations. Since the beginning, women have been considered to be inferior beings on the planet. There is a bulk of evidence to support this fact. Almost every country, no matter how developed, has had a history of women being mistreated.

Some of the obstacles faced by women population have been poverty, lack of education and employment, female infanticide, no or limited access to healthcare facilities. They have been perceived submissive and seen better in the role of a homemaker but not beyond that. While men have been perceived as the 'Karta dharta' of the family who is responsible for the family's social and economic stability. In many societies, parents depend on their son for old age as girl leaves her family and joins her husband's family when she marries, so she is more of liability for parents.

Female infanticide has been another major concern and one of the most under-report crimes. Females have often been subjected to different kinds of harm, neglect and violence in the form of abuse, harassment, domestic violence, rape, etc.

How do we change this? We as a society first and foremost need to change our narrow outlook as this is the need of the hour. This will pave the way for the empowerment of women. Whilst, many initiatives have been started by governmental and non-governmental agencies to reduce gender inequality, for instance, 'Beti Bachao Beti Padhao' was started to ensure survival, education and protection of the girl child and another initiative, 'Nirbhaya squad' which was formed to put a stop to various crimes focused against women's rights from sexual harassment, rape, acid attacks, etc, but is this enough. To what extent have we achieved success in tackling or eliminating the threats against women as most of them go unnoticed or unreported.

The progress of the nation is incomplete unless women are given equal status. Women need to be provided equal opportunities as their male counterparts on every front. Their efforts and participation need to be acknowledged and appreciated. Even though women in all fields have proven themselves as equally dynamic and competent, we are still very far from saying that women are given equal treatment in a male-dominated society.

Gender inequality continues at the workplace too. Female workers are still underpaid than their male counterparts for an equal amount of work and continue to be under-represented in senior management positions. For sustainable development, it is essential to have full participation and partnership of both men and women equally, be it responsibilities of household chores, raising kids and maintenance of the household.

In most countries, women receive less or no formal education, which leads to the loss of economy as women's knowledge, skills and abilities often go unrecognized.

Let us all bear in mind that education is one of the powerful vehicles to overcome this inequality. It is one of the most important mediums to make us understand that women can equally contribute and participate in the development process.

It is high time that countries come up together to build the system for women's equal participation and equitable representation at all levels. Government and organizations should take more ownership in eliminating all practices that discriminate against women rather than just having policies and initiatives on paper. Taking required steps to improve women's ability to earn income and ensuring women's equal access to the labour market and benefit programs are some things that need to be seriously looked into.

Women need to take inspiration from the successful women whose achievements in the various fields have brought laurels. It's high time, a change of attitude where women are regarded as the weaker being needs to change totally. She needs to be a role model for others rather than looking for a role model. They need to strongly believe themselves that they play an equally important role in the development of the economy and nation-building.

About the Author:

Ms. Bharti Paryani: Batch 2018-20

I have been in the field of education for the past 18 years and, during this period of 18 years, I have played different roles and worked with reputed IB schools. After doing my E.C.C. Ed, I started my journey as a teacher with the Early years. Subsequently, I did my B. Ed and Master's in Sociology and Literature. Being a language lover, I have enjoyed learning foreign languages like Spanish and French. Currently, I have been working as a IB PYP facilitator in JBCN international school since July 2020.

CHAPTER FOUR

MENTORING WOMEN PROFESSIONALLY AND PERSONALLY

Ms. Seema Kajale

Alumna Batch: 2011 -2012

"Every man needs a woman when his life is a mess because just like the games of chess - the Queen protects the King." Women's empowerment can be defined to promoting women's sense of self-worth, their ability to determine their own choices and their right to influence social change for themselves and others. "Whatever you fear most has no power- it is your fear that has power. " - Oprah Winfrey

Imagine a gender equal world. A world free of bias, stereotypes and discrimination. A world where difference is valued and celebrated. Together we can forge women's equality. Collectively we can all #BreakTheBias. "Women don't need to find their voices, they need to be empowered to use it and people need to be urged to listen." -Meghan Markle We need to take an action for equality. Women have been making a name for themselves in organisations all over the world. They are taking their career goals to the next level and claiming the positions they have worked very hard for. Despite this, many top positions within the organisations are still held by men. However, there is a situation to help women get into more leadership roles. It is through - Mentoring. Mentoring can help women with their career development. Here are some view points about Mentoring that can benefit women in leadership: 1. Many times, women choose to leave organisations because they do not feel like their abilities are valued by their leaders. Mentoring can help in change of this perception- by boosting her confidence. This will definitely result in developing her skills. This will help us to become a progressive nation. 2. Women are less spoken about their ambitions in the organisation. Mentoring will provide a safe space for women to openly discuss their ambitions. It will give them a much needed push in the right direction. 3. Being a part of Mentoring relationship can help to hold women accountable to their personal goals. Consistent goal achievements lead to higher performance and advancement throughout the organisation. This will help us to become a progressive nation. 4. Women tend to have fewer connections at work due to lack of networking. A mentor can introduce them to others in their profession and generally make them more visible throughout the organisation. Being in the network will promote to overcome feeling of un-awareness within the organisation. It will help them to overcome the professional and personal challenges. This change will definitely help us to become the progressive nation. 5. We all need to be more confident in our skills and abilities. So that we can take tough decisions and perform other necessary leadership tasks. Correct Mentoring will help women to gain the much needed confidence to make a move towards becoming a progressive nation. According to Forbes, Mentoring is one of the top strategies to help close the gender gap in business leadership. If, we have a female role models to emulate, it will be of a great help to boost the moral. Mentor will work like someone who will help the women by sharing their experiences and wisdom, encourages new ways of thinking, challenges the assumptions and helps to learn new skills. A mentor can be of any age, at any level and in any field. If the women in our country finds someone they admire, someone who has a professional style they want to emulate, or a skill set they want to develop - then imagine the outcome. - When women do well, so does everyone. - Constant progress - Peace in our heart, peace in the world - Dignity of labour - Together we make equality in reality - Safer and healthier communities - Equal opportunities - Epitome of sincerity, simplicity, serenity and sympathy There is no limit to what we as women can accomplish. ***"We need women at all levels, including the top, to change the dynamic, reshape the conversation, to make sure that women's voices are heard and heeded, not overlooked and ignored. " -Sheryl Sandberg***

"Every man needs a woman when his life is a mess because just like the games of chess - the Queen protects the King."

Women's empowerment can be defined to promoting women's sense of self-worth, their ability to determine their own choices and their right to influence social change for themselves and others.

"Whatever you fear most has no power- it is your fear that has power. " - Oprah Winfrey

Imagine a gender equal world. A world free of bias, stereotypes, and discrimination. A world where difference is valued and celebrated. Together we can forge women's equality. Collectively we can all #BreakTheBias.

"Women don't need to find their voices, they need to be empowered to use it and people need to be urged to listen." -Meghan Markle

We need to take an action for equality.

Women have been making a name for themselves in organisations all over the world. They are taking their career goals to the next level and claiming the positions they have worked very hard for. Despite this, many top positions within the organisations are still held by men. However, there is a situation to help women get into more leadership roles. It is through - Mentoring.

Mentoring can help women with their career development. Here are some viewpoints about Mentoring that can benefit women in leadership:

1. Many times, women choose to leave organisations because they do not feel like their abilities are valued by their leaders. Mentoring can help in change of this perception- by boosting her confidence. This will result in developing her skills. This will help us to become a progressive nation.

2. Women are less spoken about their ambitions in the organisation. Mentoring will provide a safe space for women to openly discuss their ambitions. It will give them

a much-needed push in the right direction.

3. Being a part of Mentoring relationship can help to hold women accountable to their personal goals. Consistent goal achievements lead to higher performance and advancement throughout the organisation. This will help us to become a progressive nation.

4. Women tend to have fewer connections at work due to lack of networking. A mentor can introduce them to others in their profession and generally make them more visible throughout the organisation. Being in the network will promote to overcome feeling of un-awareness within the organisation. It will help them to overcome the professional and personal challenges. This change will definitely help us to become the progressive nation.

5. We all need to be more confident in our skills and abilities. So that we can take tough decisions and perform other necessary leadership tasks. Correct Mentoring will help women to gain the much needed confidence to make a move towards becoming a progressive nation.

According to Forbes,

Mentoring is one of the top strategies to help close the gender gap in business leadership. If, we have a female role models to emulate, it will be of a great help to boost the moral.

Mentor will work like someone who will help the women by sharing their experiences and wisdom, encourages new ways of thinking, challenges the assumptions and helps to learn new skills. A mentor can be of any age, at any level and in any field.

If the women in our country finds someone they admire, someone who has a professional style they want to emulate, or a skill set they want to develop - then imagine the outcome.

- When women do well, so does everyone.

- Constant progress

- Peace in our heart, peace in the world

- Dignity of labour

- Together we make equality in reality

- Safer and healthier communities

- Equal opportunities

- Epitome of sincerity, simplicity, serenity and sympathy

There is no limit to what we as women can accomplish.

"We need women at all levels, including the top, to change the dynamic, reshape the conversation, to make sure that women's voices are heard and heeded, not overlooked and ignored. "

-Sheryl Sandberg

About the author:

Ms. Seema Kajale - Batch 2011-12

- Qualifications: M.Com, Web Designer, B. ED
- Achievements: Authored 2 books for Jeevandip Prakashan, Marathi subject std 10th Paper Solution Set.Did translation work of Marathi poems into Hindi.

CHAPTER FIVE

WOMEN AND THEIR ROLE IN THE SOCIETY

Ms. Shivani Mayekar

Alumna Batch 2019-21

"The day a woman can walk freely on the roads at night, that day we can say that India has achieved independence." – Mahatma Gandhi

Women have multiple roles to play they are daughters, granddaughters, nieces, friend, sister, wife, mother, etc. They have a role to play in the society of a docile, perfect, obedient person which they play beautifully.

A woman is by nature a nurturing person, she nurtures her children and family. Always keeping her family, friends in the forefront and herself last in the priority list, her ability to seek peace and cooperation.

Her ability to be empathetic and tolerant has been misunderstood as her weakness and society have long since oppressed and exploited women.

History has plenty of examples where women have broken free of the shackles placed by the society and rose up as beautiful phoenix, who refused to confound to the social conventions. We have had Rani Laxmi Bai, Razia Sultan, Savitri Bai Phule, Channama and many more who sacrificed their life for independence of India and women empowerment.

We have Mother Teressa, Indira Gandhi, the new age women who refused to be molded into a socially acceptable cast. They have all set an example of what a woman can achieve if she sets her mind on it. They are all prominent figures in our history books. History is not just in the past but it is a map for us to follow.

“There is no limit to what we as women can accomplish.” – Michelle Obama

No truer words uttered by none other than Michelle Obama, who successful in her own right also proved the proverb that ‘behind every successful man there is a woman.’

Women are programmed to be damsel in distress. Waiting for her brave prince to come and rescue her. Which is pretty much what is happening in all the fairytales that are read to us since childhood. Further as we grow, we have a whole bunch of Bollywood movies who reiterate the same thing, where women are helpless and need strong men to rescue them.

Thankfully newer fairytales like ‘BRAVE’ are taking place, where women are stirring their own ship.

Women are waking to protest against stereotyping and are now refusing to be reduced to being an ornament. They are staking their claim in the society, making their stamp on the map. They are making a name for themselves and their nation. We have several examples like Priyanka Chopra, Mary Kom, Kathy Lueders, Kalpana Chawla, etc. These are all famous personalities who are breaking the glass ceiling, all educated and knowledable.

There are many others who are there trying to come up or break free from the clasp of patriarchal society and their archaical laws, customs and traditions. These are women who are working at the grassroot level. They not only freed themselves of this oppression but are also helping others to become independent and empowered.

One such woman whom I have come across is Ningamma of Karnataka, who at the tender age of 15 years old realized that being Lord Hanuman's wife doesn't protect her in her darkest hours. Yes, she was a Devadasi.

Her constant thought was that no other girl should suffer as she had suffered in her life. It was in 2001, when community led initiative along with the zeal with which a federation of women was formed named, 'The Navajeevan Mahila Okkoota.' The immense success and impact of this movement was that soon about 2500 devadasis joint.

In the last two decades, 300 villages in the district are free of the Devadasi practice. During this time, it was realized that it wasn't just a case about gender issues but it had its roots deeply embedded into caste and class. All of the Devadasis were Dalits and were also from the poor families.

Upon this realization, the federation started to impart importance of education along with giving scholarship to girls to pursue in academic fields. This initiative was a grand triumph. All the children are well educated, some having admirably completed professional courses and even doctoral degree.

This was the story of one woman who wanted to free herself and along the way met likeminded women and changed the scenario of the districts nearby. This was the story of one woman who uplifted the lives of others along with eradication of stratification and marginalization of the society.

This was an example of just one such woman who became a catalyst of change in the society. The contribution of women in the transition from pre-literate to literate is undeniable.

A mother encourages her child to attend and stay in school. Also installs values in them. As the saying goes 'The hand that rocks the cradle rules the world.' Examples are Olympias, the mother of Alexander the Great, Jijabai, the mother of Chhatrapati Shivaji Maharaj.

Most important, majority of the workforce in teaching are women, women who guide the future generation and indirectly shape the generation along with future of the society. Also 45.8% of workforce comprises of women.

I would like to conclude by stating that women play an important role in the society. Their actions values are directly and indirectly are responsible for shaping the society.

About the Author:

Ms. Shivani Mayekar: Batch 2019-21

- B.A (Gold medalist), M.A (philosophy), B.Ed, Basic & Advance Diploma in Yoga, Diploma in Mythology.
- Experience of teaching 3 years as Assistant Professor in BMS Dept in D.G.Ruparel College and currently working as Assistant Professor in Department of Philosophy in G.N. Khalsa College.

CHAPTER SIX

Women Empowerment Towards a Progressive Nation

Ms. Rakhi Pande

Alumna Batch 2011 -12

Much has been written and said about empowerment of women especially on the occasion on International Women's Day each year which has generated great awareness and momentum towards a movement of breaking the gender bias. This is in fact, the theme for 2022, highlighted as #breakthebias. (IWD, 2022) While reflecting on the relevance and significance of this movement for the purpose of penning this chapter, especially when focus on global health was 'top of mind' for everyone, I wondered if this movement lost any traction and also if there was any gender bias when it came to Covid fatalities. Imagine my surprise when various sources cited that there was a gender bias. It may sound unbelievable, but global data captured in 2020 indicated that men had higher fatalities than women when it came to Covid. Imagine my shock when a further probe revealed that, bizarrely, at the same time, India was an exception to this rule! (Nabamallika Dehingia, 2020). More women were dying here. (Shetty, 2020) Could it be related to the quality or lack of care provided to one gender? This is a whole research topic in itself, however not the only objective of this chapter. Apart from women's health, when it comes to gender equality and safety, equal pay or even basic education for the girl child - at the very least, awareness about these principles for women empowerment already exists driven by the celebration of International Women's Day among other efforts. Globally, school enrollments are reaching gender parity, though, on the flip side, dropout rates are higher for girls. In India, the sex ratio has improved with 1020 girls for every 1000 boys, though the sex ratio at birth is still lower for females. (Ruchika Chitravanshi, 2021) The implications of this could be ominous based on how the data is interpreted – but again, there is already a lot of public discussion, outreach effort and material on this for India as well as other developing countries. So, instead, I would like us to reflect on deconstructing the theme of 'break the bias' to deepen understanding of the definition of women's empowerment. Women empowerment means promoting women's sense of self-worth, their ability to determine their own choices, and their right to influence social change for themselves and others. (Vision, n.d.) If you are a man reading this, think about the women in your family. Is your day-to-day interaction relating to life choices geared towards this? Let us look at an example of undermining a woman's sense of self-worth from the definition given here. I know a divorced lady who gets calls for matches from her "well-wishers" of people far below her intellectual, social or emotional or aesthetic level as they believe she should settle for anything that comes her way. The same lady enjoys a fulfilling personal and professional life and counts among her circle of friends – intelligentsia and those working in diverse corporate roles, leadership roles and people from creative backgrounds. Yet she is expected to "settle" marriage-wise for someone who would not be able to hold even one engaging conversation with her or value her achievements. Her married life in total accounts for only two and a half years, but she is defined only by that by some of the harmful backward mindsets prevalent in our country. This unconscious or conscious bias - how destructive do you think this could be to her self-worth? Fortunately, she is made of sterner stuff. Another highly accomplished lady realised over the years that she used to be biased about her own 'darker' skin colour as compared to her husband's fairer skin because of the lower expectations her own family had for her when it came to planning matrimonial alliances. Let us break that bias. When it comes to bias about a woman's ability to determine her own choices, India has shown progress by changing mindsets about male dominated career roles to include women. Again, however, individual thought processes still have a long way to go. Am sure if statistical research data is made available, it would be found that women are married off at a far younger age than men. I want you to also think about why the bias exists in our society that male spouses must be older than female ones? Why not the reverse, in that case? Let us break that bias. What about a woman's right to influence social change for herself and others? Well, I just tried doing that and am thankful for this forum given to me. Historically and in present times there are women involved in stellar efforts towards this endeavour. India has very quickly come halfway. I'm positive we will continue to change mindsets at an accelerated rate. I leave you all with a request to reflect – irrespective of your own gender – what biases you consciously or unconsciously employ with the women in your life. Empower your thinking to empower the women around you. Reach out to me if you like, with examples of how you have achieved this. How did you break the bias?

References:

IWD. (2022, March 8). *International Women's Day*. Retrieved from IWD Theme: https://www.internationalwomensday.com/Theme

Nabamallika Dehingia, A. R. (2020, November 5). *The Lancet Global Health*. Retrieved from The Lancet: https://www.thelancet.com/journals/langlo/article/PIIS2214-109X(20)30464-2/fulltext#:~:text=Global%20data%20indicate%20higher%20COVID,in%20s

Ruchika Chitravanshi, I. G. (2021, November 26). *Business Standard*. Retrieved from https://www.business-standard.com/article/current-affairs/india-now-has-more-women-than-men-but-sex-ratio-at-birth-still-low-121112501539_1.html

Shetty, D. (2020, June). *IndiaSpend.com*. Retrieved from https://www.thelancet.com/journals/langlo/article/PIIS2214-109X(20)30464-2/

fulltext#:~:text=Global%20data%20indicate%20higher%20COVID,in%20so

Vision, W. (n.d.). *World Vision Australia*. Retrieved from https://www.worldvision.com.au/womens-empowerment/#:~:text=Women's%20empowerment%20can%20be%20d

About the author

Rakhi Pande - 2011-12 B.Ed Batch of PCER

Rakhi Pande has worked with top Mumbai schools as a Secondary and Primary teaching and leadership roles across CIE, IGCSE, IPC and ICSE along with heading the English department (Primary) at a British curriculum school in Dubai, UAE and working in consultancy services. She segued into this profession after quitting her erstwhile post as General Manager in the field of brand management in India. Having spent her formative years in Mumbai she has spent a decade in each profession before exploring greener pastures abroad. An avid reader and award-winning educator, while dabbling with blogging and other creative pursuits, she writes whenever time permits. Her short stories have been published recently by Muse India and Borderless Journal.

Contact details:

- Email : rakhipande10@gmail.com
- https://www.linkedin.com/in/rakhi-pande-362a387

CHAPTER SEVEN

Women Empowerment towards a Progressive Nation

Ms. Prateeksha Pandey Goel

Alumna Batch 2015-17

We have often heard 'Behind every successful man is a woman'. This age old saying needs a drastic change with our constantly changing world. **Empowered women empower women.** Which stands true for every woman out there.

One important question that arises at this point of time is - why do we need to empower women? Aren't we living a fulfilling life-With our jobs, family, friends and of course the societal norms? All over the world women are facing threats to their lives, well-being and health due to the lack of power and influence. Women are overburdened with work be it at home, a work place or as a general role in the society. Women have been bearing the burden for the very long time.

One of the first step towards Women Empowerment would be Education. Education helps women gain self-awareness, develop an understanding of the self and gain knowledge, skills and confidence. An educated women will be aware of her rights. She will have the confidence to control her life. At the same time make educated and informed choices both from within and outside of her home.

Educated women help themselves by raising their status in the society. Literacy helps women make life-determining decisions through the problems in the society. Due to the ability and capabilities that an empowered/ educated woman has it enables them, with the freedom to pursue desired goals. This in turn not only leads to the personal development of an individual but also contributes to the development of the society in terms of socio-economic development.

Empowered women not only have the ability to control their lives but also take part and control the resources, income and assets. An educated women has more say in different aspects of the life. This allows them to redefine gender roles in the society. Such participation in the society leads to empowerment of women.

An empowered women will not only work towards her upliftment in the society but also help others. For instance, if we take the simple example of our homes – girls look up to their mother, aunts or sisters. Now if the women of the family are uneducated and lack any kind of role in the decision making of the family. Then this in turn sets the motion of unawareness, over load of work and lack of self-confidence.

If we change the above scenario with one factor that is the women of the family are well educated and empowered. They are constantly involved in the decision making of the family. They are aware of their self-worth and have jobs. This will in turn set the motion of positive attitude towards self-confidence, self-awareness, learning, knowledge and skills.

The above example although of a simple household but reinstates a very important point of empowered women empower women. Be that women who is not only empowered but also actively participates in empowering other women; be it a work place, our homes or schools. It's the small step take will lead to a holistic development of the society as a whole.

About the Author:

Ms. Prateeksha Pandey Goel: Batch 2015-17

Prateeksha Pandey Goel fueled by her passion for teaching and learning. She is the chairman of Al Shatir Children Skills Development Center. She has prior experience of teaching at Dubai Scholars Private School. She considers herself a 'forever student,' eager to build on her academic foundations in the field of education. Her background in B. and B.Ed. informs her mindful but competitive approach.

CHAPTER EIGHT

WOMEN EMPOWERMENT TOWARDS A PROGRESSIVE NATION

Ms. Alisha Memon

Alumna Batch: 2019-2021

"There is no limit to what we, as women, can accomplish."

-Michelle Obama

Women empowerment indicates addressing women's power to create them proficient in taking decisions for themselves. Women have undergone a lot over the years in this man-dominating world. In more primitive centuries, they were treated as almost non-existent human beings. As if whole rights belonged to men even the basic right such as voting. As time unfolded, women understood their power. Since then, the revolution for women empowerment started in this world.

Women empowerment is the process that creates power in women to live a happy and respectable life in a society. Women are empowered when they can access opportunities in a variety of fields such as education, awareness, literacy, and training. Women's empowerment is the most crucial point for the overall development of a country. According to History, women were ill-treated through practices like Sati, girl child abortion and women continue facing issues such as violence, acid attacks and rapes. Due to practices like female foeticide, girl child numbers are decreasing in India which has impacted the sex ratio and the literacy rate among girls is very low. Most of the girls do not even get primary education and are forced to marry at an early age. Even at workplace, women are discriminated against men.

Women can be empowered through government schemes as well as on individual basis. At individual level, we should start respecting women and start giving them opportunities equal to men. We must promote and encourage them to take up jobs, higher education, business activities etc. The family members of women also need to be made aware about the importance of empowering women as society and family contribute a lot to this cause. We can also empower women by abolishing social evils like the dowry system, child marriage. The Government has come up with various schemes such as Beti Bachao Beti Padhao Yojana, Ahila-E-Haat, Mahila Shakti Kendra, Working women Hostel, Sukanya Samriddhi Yojana etc.

These small steps will change the situation of women in society and make them feel empowered.

CHAPTER NINE

Women Empowerment towards a Progressive Nation

Ms. Nikita Tikhe

Alumna Batch: 2015-2017

Empowerment' refers to the ability of a person from which one gets this ability in which he/she can take all the decisions related to his/her life.

Women empowerment refers to making women powerful to make them capable of deciding for themselves. Women have suffered a lot through the years at the hands of men. In earlier centuries, they were treated as almost non-existent. As if all the rights belonged to men even something as basic as voting. As the time evolved, women realized their power. There on began the revolution for women empowerment.

India is a democratic country. Today, India is competing with the world economy, but the condition of women is same as it was before independence. Indian society is still a patriarchal society. Till date, male dominance is prevailing in India. Women are still given secondary status in the Indian society. We still have a long way to go when we talk about the reasons why we need women empowerment.

Almost every country, no matter how progressive has a history of ill-treating women. In other words, women from all over the world have to struggle hard to reach the status they have today. Country like India still lack behind in Women Empowerment. In India, women empowerment is needed more than ever.

Laxmi Agarwal is an Indian acid attack survivor. She leads a campaign for the rights of acid attack victims. She is also a famous TV host.

She is one of the best examples when we talk about women empowerment towards progress in India as Laxmi Agarwal been honoured with the international women empowerment award from the ministry of women and child development and **UNICEF** for her campaign of *'Stop Acid Sale'* in 2019. Under the new regulation, acid could not be sold to any individual below the age of 18 yrs. It is also made compulsory to present a photo identity card before buying acid.

Moreover, the education and freedom scenario is very regressive here. Women are not allowed to pursue higher education; they are married-off early.

Here, we can throw some light on the life of **Late Sindhutai Sakpal** who gave her entire life to orphans. For which, she was called as *Mai* (mother). She has

nurtured more than 1,050 orphaned children. She is an *Indian Social Worker, Social Entrepreneur and Social Activist* known for her work for orphan children in India and won 700 awards.

There are various ways how one can empower women. The individuals and government must both come together to make it happen.

Laxmi Narayan Tripathi famously known as Laxmi a *Transgender* is another famous personality who has been representing India in different countries when we talk about women empowerment.

She is a *Transgender Rights Activist, Bharatanatyam Dancer, Choreographer & Motivational Speaker*. She has been declared as **Acharya Mahamandaleshwar** of **Kinnar Akhada.**

Laxmi has served on the boards of several NGOs which *conducts LGBT activist work*. In 2002, she became President of the **NGO DAI Welfare Society**, the first registered & working organisation for eunuchs in South Asia. In 2007, she started her own organization, 'Astitva'. This organization works to promote the welfare of sexual minorities, their support and development. In April 2014, Indian Supreme Court recognized transgender rights, officially recognizing them as the third gender in India. With this recognition the courts have ordered the Government to provide quotas in jobs and education.

The famous quote by **Pandit Jawaharlal Nehru**, *"To awaken people, women must be awakened"*. To empower women, first, it is necessary to kill those demonic thoughts that kill their rights and values in a society like a dowry, illiteracy, sexual violence, inequality, foeticide, domestic violence, rape, prostitution, human trafficking & similar topics. Gender discrimination brings socio-economic cultural & educational differences in the nation which puts the country backwards. Empowering women to ensure the right to equality mentioned in the Constitution of India is the most effective way to eradicate such evils.

Giving priority to gender equality has promoted women empowerment across India. To achieve the high goal of women empowerment, it should be propagated & broadcasted in every family from childhood. A better education can start at home from childhood, a healthy family is needed for the upliftment of women which is necessary for the all-round development of the nation.

About the Author:

Ms. Nikita Vinayak Kshirsagar : Batch 2015-17

Qualifications-B. A (Economics); M.A; B.Ed (History);PET

Presently teaching at Chembur English High School and Junior college. My work experience includes teaching at institutions such as O.L.P.S School, Maharshi Dayanand College of Arts Science and Commerce, Vivekanand Education Society. I enjoy teaching very much. I learned many new things from different institutions where I have worked. Working with experienced teachers and professors helped me to explore more and improve a lot in my work. I believe learning takes place anywhere from anyone. I aim to learn as much as I can and serve the society well.

CHAPTER TEN

WOMEN WILL RULE THE WORLD!

Ms. Bhakti Gala

Alumna Batch: 2017-2019

"The Rise of the Women = The Rise of a Nation".

For thousands of years, India has been a patriarchal society which has treated woman like a showpiece in the house, who could not voice out her opinions, feelings, thoughts and also was expected to follow what the men in the family told her to. You can break down a woman temporarily but a real women will always pick up the pieces, rebuild herself and comeback stronger than ever. History has witnessed many such examples like Rani Laxmibai, Mother Teresa, Savitribai Phule, Kasturba Gandhi, Pandita Ramabai, Kiran Bedi, Jhulan Goswami, to name a few.

Let us evaluate the journey of women across generations in various walks of life and the future they behold. To start with, let me highlight the life of Rani Laxmibai, we all know her as a fierce woman. After the death of her husband, she fought with the Britishers with a small kid on her back. Jhansi ki Rani – Rani Lakshmi Bai, who fought for her Dharma, is known even today as a brave queen and is often referred to as 'Khub Ladi Mardani, woh to Jhanisiwali Rani Thi!'.

Another powerful woman who fought for the rights of the people in the society was Mother Teresa. Mother Teresa contributed to the elevation of many people's daily miseries. However, her way of life was not free from criticism. Despite all the ambiguities surrounding her, her example will live on and encourage the people of the world to do better for themselves and for the people around them.

Our motherland India's another influential daughter is Dr. Kiran Bedi. She became the first woman Indian Police Service (IPS) Officer by clearing the highly competent Indian Civil Services Examination. She underwent training at the National Academy of Administration in Mussoorie where she was the only woman in a batch of 80 men. She was awarded the president's police medal for gallantry in 1979. She was the first Indian woman to be appointed civilian police advisor in U.N.

"Empowering a woman is key to building a future that we want."- Amartya Sen. The women of today are becoming more independent, fierce and powerful than ever before. The role of women in current society is dynamic. They are expected to not only to cook but are also encouraged to fight for the county. This can be evidently seen in the change in the role of women in the armed forces. Women initially were allowed to take up only desk jobs or non-combatant roles in the defence forces. From 2020, women were inducted into more combatant roles like Army

Aviation Corps, Army Service Corps, Corps of Army Defence, Intelligence Corps, to name a few. Gunjan Saxena, Padmavatht Bandopadhyay, Mitali Madhumita are few women from the defence forces who have risen up, fought with the society and achieved glory for themselves and our country.

A woman today is not only expected to be dolled up all the time, she is encouraged, inspired to take up the sports field, train in the sun and mud and win many laurels for the country. Sania Mirza, Saina Nehwal, Jhulan Goswami, Mithali Raj, etc. have fought against all criticisms and achieved great success in the respective fields motivating the next generation sports stars like Shefali Varma, Richa Gosh and many many others to take up sports as a full-time career.

The present-day woman's role does not end in home administration and management. She has gone way above entering into the arena of company management. Some examples of women who have taken up corporate jobs, gone up the ladder to become CEO, COO or even become founders of companies are Vandana Luthra (Founder at VLCC), Aditi Gupta (Founder of Menstrupedia), Falguni Nayar (Founder of Nykaa), Kiran Mazumdar Shaw (Founder of Biocon Limited). These women not only aspired to achieve big in their lives but also worked for the growth of other budding women entrepreneurs by either funding them or motivating them.

In India, a girl is considered as 'Laxmi' (goddess of money) but when she speaks about finances, a woman is always mocked. But now the time has changed and Ms. Nirmala Sitharaman who is an economists and politician is the currently serving as Minister of Finance and Corporate Affairs of India. Many women today are taking up politics, holding prominent and promising ministries of the country. All the above examples highlight the fact that women are no less than men, they are superior and here to prove nothing is impossible for them. Coming years will see women become best leaders, achievers, sports personalities, financial advisors, architect, engineers, doctors, CEOs, majors, lieutenants, etc.

The future belongs to the female!!!!

Reference:

https://kiranbedi.com/about-me/

https://ivypanda.com/essays/the-life-and-work-of-mother-teresa/

https://www.hindujagruti.org/articles/29_rani-lakshmi-bai.html

https://learnodo-newtonic.com/kiran-bedi-achievements

https://byjus.com/current-affairs/women-in-the-indian-armed-forces/

About the Author:

Ms. Bhakti Gala: Batch 2017-19

Ms. Bhakti Gala is a faculty, teacher training at SIES Institute of Comprehensive Education since the last 3 years. She trains individuals to become preschool teachers. She is currently pursuing her Masters in education (M. Ed) and has completed Bachelors in education (B.Ed.), Masters in Commerce, Post Graduate Diploma in Early Childhood Education (PGDECE) and BMS. She has co-authored a book on Decoding SDG in Classroom- A Teacher's Handbook- Lesson plan on SDG. She also has 2 years of teaching experience in the pre-primary section.

CHAPTER ELEVEN

Women Empowerment Towards a Progressive Nation

Ms. Alphonsa Shanti

Alumna Batch: 2018-2020

"Women is the builder and molder of a nation's destiny. Though delicate and soft as lily, she has a heart, far stronger and bolder than of man... she is supreme inspiration of man's onward march."

-RabindranathTagore

We all celebrate Women's Day and show our appreciation for the women folk through our Facebook &

Instagram posts, WhatsApp statuses, advertisements, banners and so on...about how we cherish and respect them. In our country, we consider women as Goddesses – in the form of Laxmi, Saraswati, so on and so forth.

But is this the real face of women in our country?

Do you know that India ranks 6th among the top 10 countries with high rate of child marriages among women? Not only that, according to another survey, India languishes at the bottom five...when it comes to discrimination against women.

Being a woman in India can be fraught with difficulties. Right from birth through adulthood and into old age, women have to face several kinds of discrimination. Many social evils hold back women from reaching their true potential. Some of the prevalent heinous evils include female infanticide, female foeticide, child marriages, sex-selective abortions, illiteracy, dowry, and harassment, which are regularly inflicted upon women. Thus, we see how women empowerment is the need of the hour. We need to empower these women to speak up for themselves and encourage them to not be a victim of injustice.

There are various ways in how one can empower women. The individuals and government, both, must come together to make it happen. Education for girls must be made compulsory so that women can become literate to make a life for themselves.

Women must be given equal opportunities in every field, irrespective of gender. Moreover, they must also be given equal pay. We can empower women by abolishing child marriage.

Various programs must be held where they can be taught life skills to fend for themselves in case they ever face a financial crisis. Most importantly, the shame of divorce and abuse of any sort, must be abolished for good. Many women stay in abusive relationships because of the fear of society.

Parents must teach their daughters it is okay to come home divorced...rather than returning home in a coffin.

Women need to take inspiration from the top Indian women whose achievements in various fields have brought laurels - For instance:

Rani Rampal, Indian Hockey Team Captain - She has suffered poverty as well as taunts of relatives and society. Relatives also used to taunt her father and say, 'What will she do by playing hockey? Just wearing a short skirt, will run in the field and ruin the honor of the house'. At that time, she was afraid that she would never be able to play hockey. Today, the same set of people praise her and visit her place when she returns home.

Laxmi Agarwal, Acid Victim - She suffered serious burns from acid thrown on her just because she refused to marry a 32-old person when she was just 15 years of age. She bounced back with double courage and still inspires all of us. Laxmi has also received the 'International Women Empowerment Award 2019' from the Ministry of Women and Child Development.

Gunjan Saxena, 1st Indian female pilot in combat - She became 'Kargil Girl' by flying fighter jets among boys and created history by doing so, and set an example for the future generations.

Geeta & Babita Phogat, Wrestlers - When these Dangal Girls fought boys to learn the game.

All these inspiring stories tell how these women fought against the stereotypical society and rose from the ashes.

Thus we can conclude that women empowerment is a process, not a product. There has been immense progress to uplift women financially, politically and socially; but it is still an open-ended process. A concerted and coordinated effort is required from all quarters to change women's present circumstances. A change of social attitude which regards women as the weaker sex, is essential. Instead of looking for role models, she needs to be a role model for others. Women need to have this conviction they are an asset to our country and form the cornerstone, when it comes to nation-building.

About the Author:

Ms. Alphonsa Shanthi: Batch 2018-20

Completed my MA in English from the University of Mumbai and B. Ed from Pillai college of Education and Research, Chembur. I am presently working as an assistant teacher for the past 7 years at Sharadashram Vidyamandir English Medium High School, Dadar.

CHAPTER TWELVE

Women Empowerment Towards a Progressive Nation

Ms. Cristin Kenny

Alumna Batch: 2019-2021

Sarojini Naidu. When India was writhing under the shackles of the British rule, trying its best to break free, Sarojini Naidu made her way into the U.S to promote Nonviolent Resistance. It was during the time when powerful countries such as England and America were contemplating giving their women the right to vote that India took this bold chance and sent the first female president of the Indian National Congress as its representative seven seas across. This to me, is the strongest example of women empowerment towards a progressive nation.

In layman's language, to empower means to vest power and to be progressive means to develop for the better over time. To me, empowerment of women does not mean just this, rather it means to acknowledge and accept the power and skills that women possess. But how are the women of a developing country such as ours empowered? Long gone are the days when women yearned for power and had to fight for it. Today, we see special reservations made for women in all fields starting from public vehicles to the parliament. Women are given privileges and encouraged to come forth and actively participate. For aeons, battles have been fought to bring women to the forefront of the nation; to give them voice and these efforts have borne fruit. Starting with the late Indira Gandhi who used to make important decisions for our country's future to Gunjan Saxena who played an important role in the Kargil war to Priyanka Chopra who became the face of India for international media, our country has proudly and respectfully empowered women throughout the years.

Such recognitions and attributions given to our ladies is concurrently increasing and shaping our country's identity. Today, India is among the top sought after nations thanks to its passionate, resilient and purpose driven iron ladies among the many eminent personalities. I, right from school till college, have been mentored and guided by Amazon like stalwarts who have scaled their institutions to great heights. From them I learned the power and prowess a woman holds. And from the men in my life, I learned that all human beings, irrespective of their gender, must be treated with dignity and respect.

The world today is a much better place, surely, but there is still room for progress, and we women want to be a part of driving it. For this, we will continue to strive and do everything in our power to leave the world a better place than we found it.

About the Author:

Ms. Cristin Kenny: Batch 2019-21

Current designation: Primary/ middle school teacher at the Green Acres Academy, Chembur.

Educational qualification: B. A in English Literature and B.Ed., currently pursuing M.A in English

Authors

Article: She and We
Dr. Reni Francis - Principal, MES's Pillai College of Education and Research, Chembur

Article: Gender Equality- Empowering the other half of the Nation Builders
Dr. Jaya Cherian - Asst. Professor, MES's Pillai College of Education and Research, Chembur

Article: Women Empowerment towards a Progressive Nation
Ms. Bharti Paryani - Alumna PCER, Chembur 2019-21

Article: Mentoring women professionally and personally
Ms. Seema Kajale - Alumna PCER, Chembur 2011 - 2012

Article: Women and their Role in the Society
Ms. Shivani Mayekar - Alumna PCER, Chembur 2019-21

Article: Women Empowerment Towards a Progressive Nation
Ms. Rakhi Pande - Alumna PCER, Chembur 2011-12

Article: Women Empowerment towards a Progressive Nation
Ms. Prateeksha Pandey Goel - Alumna PCER, Chembur 2015-17

Article: Women Empowerment Towards a Progressive Nation
Ms. Alisha Memon - Alumna PCER, Chembur 2019 - 2021

Article: Women Empowerment Towards a Progressive Nation
Ms. Nikita Tikhe - Alumna PCER, Chembur 2011-12

Article: Women will Rule the World!
Ms. Bhakti Gala - Alumna PCER, Chembur 2017-19

Article: Women Empowerment towards a Progressive Nation
Ms. Alphonsa Shanti- Alumna PCER, Chembur 2018-20

Article: Women Empowerment towards a Progressive Nation
Ms. Cristin Kenny - Alumna PCER, Chembur 2019 - 2021

Printed by Libri Plureos GmbH in Hamburg,
Germany